DAY TRADING SYSTEMS & METHODS

CHARLES LE BEAU

DAVID W. LUCAS

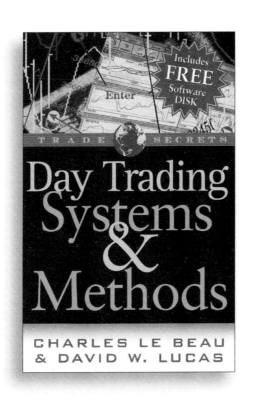

Includes
FREE
Software
DISK

Enter

T R A D E   S E C R E T S

Day Trading
Systems
&
Methods

CHARLES LE BEAU
& DAVID W. LUCAS

> This book, along with other books, are available at discounts that
> make it realistic to provide them as gifts to your customers,
> clients, and staff. For more information on these long lasting,
> cost effective premiums, please call John Boyer at 800-424-4550
> or email him at john@traderslibrary.com.

ISBN 1-883272-27-0

Printed in the United States of America.

CONTENTS

CONTENTS

BUSINESS

The day trader enters and exits trades during the same market session, normally a period of only four to six hours from opening to close. The very short-term nature of day trading presents advantages and disadvantages to the trader. The major advantages are the lower margin requirements and the absence of overnight risk. The disadvantages are the bad odds, the time and effort required, the limited profit potential, and the burdensome costs of frequent transactions.

The transaction costs consist of commissions and slippage. The trader might have a mental image of trading at the prices shown on a computer screen, but in reality she must continuously buy at the offered price and sell at the bid price. The spread between the bid and offer becomes a substantial hidden cost of doing business. It is also unrealistic to expect stop orders to be filled at the stop price all of the time. The commissions are a large and much more obvious cost. In the meantime, to offset these unavoidable costs, the day trader is limited to only very small profits. Under even the most optimistic scenario, the day trader's potential profits are limited to only a portion of the price range occurring within one day of trading.

Let us assume that our day trader is paying $20 per trade in commission, and the spread between the bid and offer amounts to $10 buying and $10 selling. For the trader to complete a trade that nets $100, she must be smart enough to identify a move of $140 on the price screen that she watches. On the other hand, when her timing is wrong by only $140, she is going to lose $180. It doesn't take a Ph.D. in mathematics to figure this isn't an ideal business environment. In fact, even the professionals on the floors of the exchanges must be excellent, highly disciplined traders just to survive. The public does not realize how many of these professionals fail, in spite of the advantage of being on the floor and paying only minimal costs per trade. Imagine how small the odds for an off-the-floor be for an off-the-floor trader faced with the costs we have described.

To have any hope of success, the day trader must strive to maximize the profits on each trade so that he can overcome the tremendous disadvantage of the transaction costs. Unfortunately, the day trader has very little control of the potential profit to be obtained, because the price range during the day so severely limits the maximum profit to be realized on an average trade. No trader can reasonably expect to buy at exact bottoms or sell at exact tops. A very good trader might hope to be able to capture the middle third of an intraday price swing. This means that to make $180 the total price swing must be three times this amount, or $540. How many futures markets have a daily price range of $540 or more? Very few. How many futures markets can produce a $180 net loss? Almost any of them.

Don't forget, the trader who is smart enough to find markets with $540 price swings and then smart enough to trade them so correctly that he nets $180 is only going to break even unless he has more winners than losers. To make money in the long run, the day trader must have a percentage of winning trades that is far better than 50 percent or he must somehow figure out how to make more than $180 on a $540 price swing. (Or best of all, do both.) This also assumes that the trader is smart and disciplined enough to harness his instincts and emotions and carefully limit the size of the losses.

TOUGH ODDS

As you can see, a day trader is faced with an almost impossible task. We would venture a very educated guess that less than one out of a thousand day traders makes money over any sustained time. Our advice is to not even attempt it. Your time and energy will be much better spent perfecting your longer-term trading skills. Even if you should succeed at day trading, it is difficult to reinvest the profits and continue to compound them. Day traders can only operate efficiently in small size, so don't expect to make your fortune at it–it's only a hard-earned living at best.

In spite of our sincere warning, we know many traders will attempt to beat the odds and become day traders for a while. Fortunately, the lessons learned can be applied to more serious and productive trading later on. We will do our best to teach you as much as we can about day trading and make the learning process less costly. Obviously, we don't have all the answers or we wouldn't have such a negative outlook on the probability of success. We have learned a great deal about this subject over many years of trading, and the fact that we have elected to no longer play this game simply demonstrates our personal preferences in the allocation of our productive time. We hope whatever hard-earned information we pass along proves helpful.

SELECTION OF MARKETS FOR DAY TRADING

As we pointed out earlier, very few markets have wide enough intraday price swings to make them suitable candidates for day trading. Day traders generally prefer to concentrate their efforts on only one or two markets. The prices must be watched closely, and there are very few markets that are suitable even if we had the capacity to follow lots of them.

Presently, day traders tend to favor the stock indexes, bonds, currencies, and energy markets. From time to time other markets may become candidates for day trading, because of temporary periods of high volatility.

We ran a test to see what percentage of the time various markets had a total daily range of $500 or more between the high of the day and the low. Here are some sample results over our most recent 1,000 days of data: S&P Index 69 percent, NY Composite 64 percent, British pounds 53 percent, T-bonds 50 percent, Swiss francs 50 percent, Japanese yen 38 percent, heating oil 37 percent, D-marks 35 percent, crude oil 31 percent, soybeans 28 percent, silver 23 percent, gold 21 percent, and sugar 13 percent. As you can see, only five markets had a $500 range 50 percent of the time.

CONSIDER TICK SIZES

In addition to looking for a wide daily range, the liquidity and the size of the minimum spread should also be factors to consider when selecting markets for day trading. Our example of costs included paying a spread of only $10 on each side of a trade. In the S&P market, a minimum spread would be $25 each side, while in the bond market a 1/32 spread is $31.25. If you are day trading bonds with $20 commissions, you must overcome total costs of $82.50 added to losses and subtracted from gains. Your average winning trade must run $165 farther than your average loss just to break even. This assumes a one tick spread, which is the best case possible. The element of liquidity comes in to play in determining the number of ticks in the spread between bid and offer. A one tick spread is the best you can hope for, and most markets have a wider spread than that. You can usually assume that the higher the average daily volume, the tighter the spread. For that reason, you will want to concentrate your day trading in only those markets with very high volume. Otherwise, you can be making good timing decisions and still be assured of losing money.

MAXIMIZING PROFITS

Day traders are constantly faced with the problem of capturing as much profit as possible from a relatively small range of prices. This situation naturally leads traders into the strategy of buying dips and selling rallies, rather than attempting to follow trends. Most trend-following strategies tend to be much too slow for day trading. Countertrend strategies offer the potential of extracting the greatest profit from a small range of prices. However, countertrend strategies tend to be less reliable than trend-following strategies, because quickly spotting turning points in prices is much more difficult than simply trading in the direction of a trend.

We have observed that the best day traders incorporate elements of both methods. Successful day traders try to buy dips within an uptrend and to sell rallies within a downtrend. The day trader who consistently makes money must be good at following trends and be good at finding short-term turning points. Most traders lose money because they are never very good at either task. As we look at some examples of possible day-trading strategies, keep these two steps in mind: First find the intermediate trend and then find the short-term turning points. Both steps need to be done quickly and accurately to produce a winning day.

OUR DISCLAIMER

The day-trading methods that follow are a few of the many methods that have been shared with us over the last few years. We seldom attempt to day trade, so we have very little first-hand experience with any of these methods. The various traders who shared these methods with us claimed success with them. We tried to select the ones that seemed most logical and the ones that seemed to hold up under a cursory examination over very limited data. The inclusion of these methods should not be considered an endorsement or recommendation. At best they should give the reader some food for thought–and a representative sample of the many methods and tools that can be used for day trading. Use them at your own risk.

THE 5-25 ENV

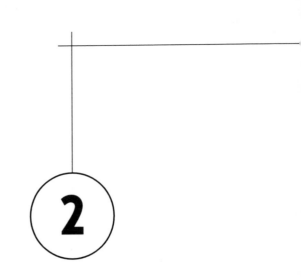

2

OPE METHOD

T his day-trading method is based on a very unusual way of using a moving average envelope. Most envelope systems call for trading in the same direction as the envelope breakout. The 5-25 method does just the opposite.

We assume that the market will traverse back and forth between the extremes of the envelope. We treat the excursions beyond the boundaries as overbought or oversold levels. After a move outside the envelope, we expect the market to re-enter the envelope and traverse to the opposite side. Here are the rules:

1. Use 30-minute bars on the S&P futures.

2. Set up an envelope study for five periods, normal (no smoothing), and at a distance of 25/100 of 1 percent from the closes.

3. Look for trades only when the boundaries of the envelope are at least 150 points apart. When one of the 30-minute bars closes at least 5 points outside the envelope, look to initiate a trade in the opposite direction as soon as the next bar closes back inside the envelope.

4. Use an initial stop loss at the extreme high or low point just before your entry. After the market has moved 75 points in your favor, the stop loss should be changed to at least your break-even point.

5. Take profits when the market reaches the opposite side of the envelope. If you want to simplify the profit taking, use the boundary of the envelope at the time you enter the trade as the target, otherwise you might have to adjust your exit point every half hour. (See Exhibit 1.)

With some modifications to the envelope, this system can be used for regular trading instead of day trading. We used to have good results using it to trade soybeans.

EXHIBIT I

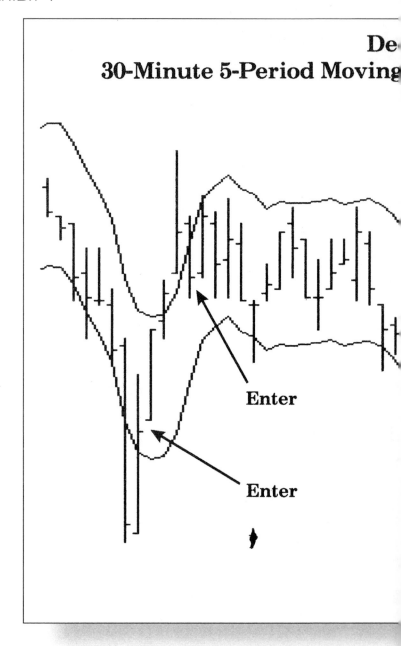

De
30-Minute 5-Period Moving

Enter

Enter

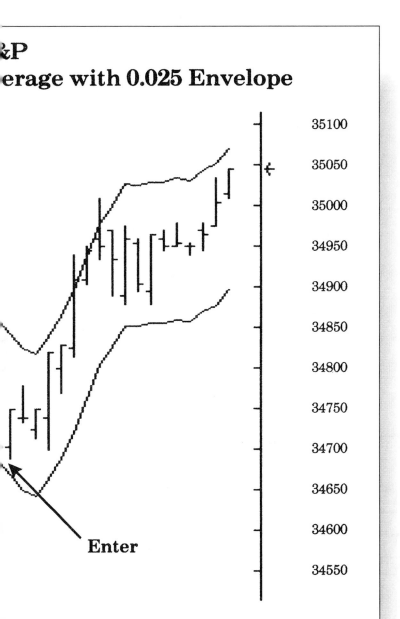

&P
erage with 0.025 Envelope

35100

35050

35000

34950

34900

34850

34800

34750

34700

34650

34600

34550

Enter

THE "HI MOM

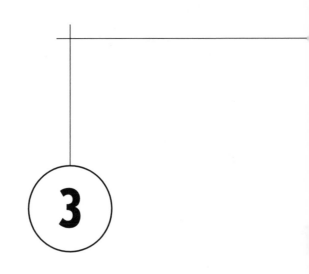

3

SYSTEM

e call this day-trading strategy the "Hi MOM" system, because trades are signaled only when there is a high momentum reading. Here is how it works:

1. Use 9-minute bars on the S&P futures. We picked the 9-minute interval because the system must be sensitive to minor price patterns. The 9-minute bars also divide the trading day into 45 equal time periods. Ten-minute bars would probably work just as well; but we have a slight preference for the logic of having all bars represent an equal time period, rather than having an odd bar at the end of the day. The 9-minute bars also give us a head start on traders using the more common intervals of 10, 15, 20, and 30 minutes.

2.   Directly underneath the 9-minute S&P bars, set up a six-bar momentum study. Scale the study so you can easily tell when the momentum reaches +/- 150.

3.   Look for divergences between the MOM study and the S&P bar chart. The first spike of the particular divergences we are looking for will have to have penetrated the +/- 150 level on our MOM chart. The second or third divergence spike does not have to reach the 150 level.

4.   After a Hi MOM divergence, enter the market as soon as possible after the hook that completes the divergence pattern. Place an initial stop loss 20 points beyond the recent high or low of the bar chart. (Point B of an AB divergence). Trail the stop using peaks and valleys on the bar chart as support and resistance levels.

5.   Take profits when there is a divergence in the opposite direction, but do not reverse the trade. We want to only trade the first divergence of the day. The exception to the one trade per day rule is when the divergence sets up as an ABC divergence with three spikes instead of two. If we entered after the second peak and were unfortunate enough to get stopped out on the third spike, we will want to initiate a second

trade in the same direction if the divergence continues. Close out any remaining open positions at the end of the day. (See Exhibit 2.)

The "Hi MOM" system is simple but very effective, because it combines the patience of waiting for volatile periods (indicated by the + /-150 MOM) with the excellent entry timing provided by divergences.

EXHIBIT 2

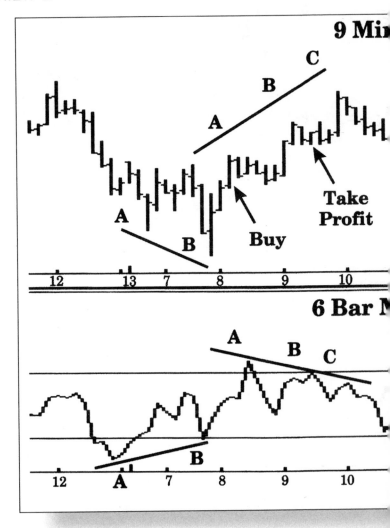

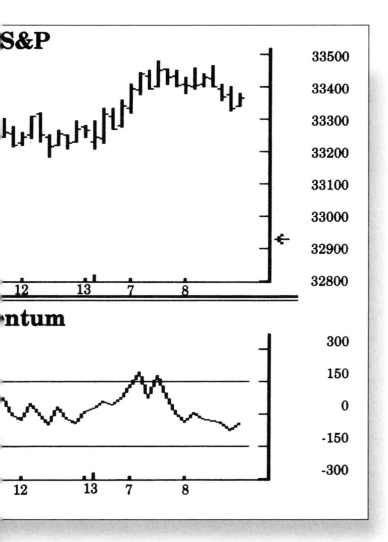

INTERMARKET
OHAMA'S 3-D TECI

4

IVERGENCES,
IQUE

One of our subscribers in the Los Angeles area, Gary Inouye, worked closely with Bill Ohama for several years prior to Bill's death in 1990.

Gary has been very successful in applying Bill's well-known "3-D" techniques to day trading. Here is an explanation:

1. Make a page of five-minute charts on two or three related commodities. For example, compare the five-minute charts of the S&P, the NY Composite, and the Major Market Index. You might also compare the T-bonds, the T-notes, and the muni bonds. There are other possible related groups, like currencies, energy futures, or the soybean complex, but the best day trades are usually in stock indexes or bonds .

2.   Carefully compare the five-minute charts for divergences where one commodity makes a new high or low and where one or more of the other commodities in the group fails to confirm by also making a new high or low. (See Exhibit 3 & 4.)

3.   When a divergence is spotted, the trade should be implemented in the most tradeable (most liquid) commodity in the group. For example, in the stock indexes you would trade the S&P, not the Major Market Index.

4.   Once a trade has been entered, some method of trailing stops would be advisable. For example, a trailing stop of about 125 points in the S&P would be a starting point. It would be logical to use wider stops during volatile periods and tighter stops when the markets are quiet.

5.   If you get a quick profit of $500 within a half hour, just take it. If the trade moves more slowly, hold on as long as it seems to be trending in the right direction. Gary does not wait for a signal to close out the trade but uses his judgment on when to take profits or losses.

This method is not a complete system, because of the lack of specific stops and the lack of a more specific exit strategy. Your results might be better or worse depending on your skill at exits. We like the entry method.

EXHIBIT 3

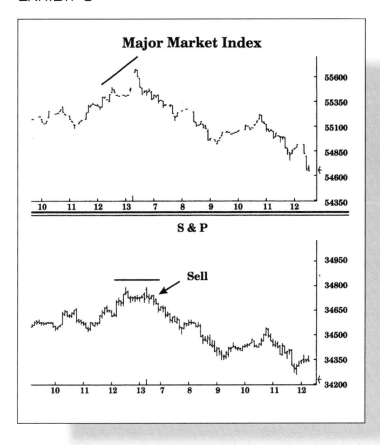

EXHIBIT 4

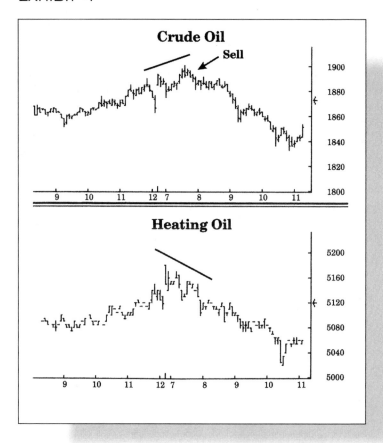

KANE'S %K HC

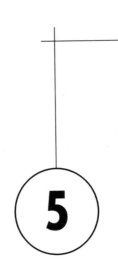

The following S&P day-trading strategy was related to us by Steve Kane, who was a fellow speaker at Fred Brown's Technical Analysis Conference in Austin, Texas, in 1990. When we returned from the seminar, we started watching the system and we have been encouraged by its effectiveness over recent data. Here is how it works:

1. Determine the trend using one-hour charts. Trade only when the hourly chart has made a higher high or lower low within the last two hours. When the trend is up, look for buy signals only. When the trend is down, look for sell signals only.

Entries: Use a five-minute chart with a 12-period slow stochastics.

Buy when the %K (the faster moving line) goes below 20 and turns up. Sell short when the %K goes above 80 and turns down. (Don't forget to trade only in the same direction as the hourly trend.)

3. Stops: Use an initial stop of 100 points, or put a closer stop just beyond a recent trading range. When the trade is 100 points ahead, it is a good idea to raise the stop to break even.

4. Exits: Take profits when the %K hooks in the opposite direction from + 80 or - 20. Another strategy is to watch the one-minute stochastics and exit whenever there is a divergence against the current trend. (See Exhibit 5 & 6.)

Steve had a few additional comments worth passing along. He has observed that, when the %K entry signals are also divergences from the price action, the resulting moves are particularly strong. He also suggests that, when there is a very sudden profit move of 100 points or more, it is often a good idea to take the profit immediately. Finally, he cautions that, whenever there are two consecutive losses in a day, it is time to stop trading and try again tomorrow. This is good advice for almost any day-trading method.

We like the idea that this is a method that buys dips in an uptrend and vice versa. We also like the idea of buying when the %K hooks, rather than waiting for the usual crossover signal. We think Steve's strategy might also be applied to day trading in other markets as well as S&Ps.

EXHIBIT 5

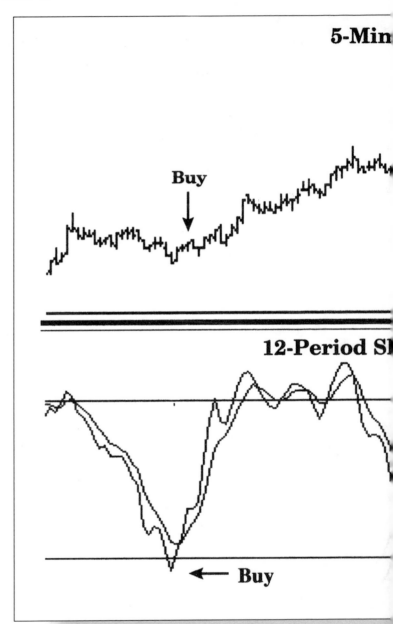

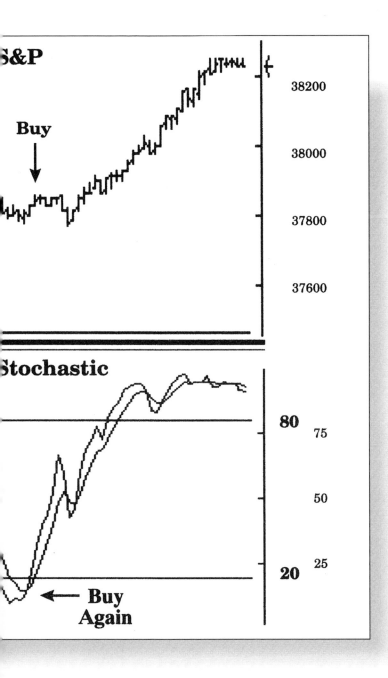

EXHIBIT 6

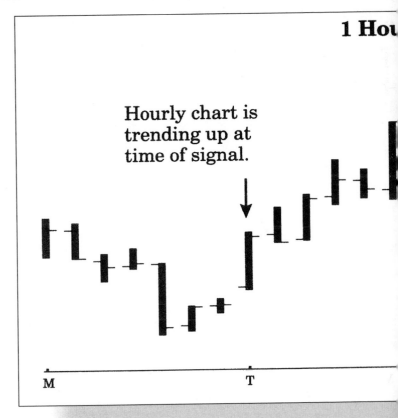

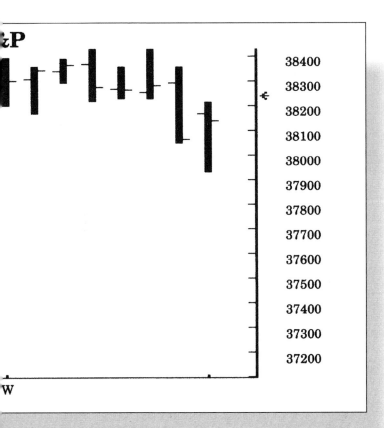

ONE-MINUTE
WITH STOCHASTIC

┫ARTS

This is a day-trading method developed by Humphrey Chang, a trader and former futures broker in California. Humphrey explained that the method works best for day trading S&P futures, but mentioned that he sometimes uses it for day trading yen and Swiss franc futures. Here is the method:

1. Use one-minute bars for the S&P futures and a 21-period stochastic.

2. One of the most important rules is that entries are done only in the first hour of trading. After the opening, wait until both stochastics lines go to an extreme level (above 80 or below 20) and then cross. Enter as quickly as possible after the cross. Ignore all other stochastics signals after the first hour.

3. Trail stops using swing patterns. Look for patterns of higher lows, or, if you are short, look for patterns of lower highs. Humphrey cautioned not to have any stops at the exact high or low of the day. He has observed these are points that the floor traders are watching and seem to raid as frequently as possible.

4. The trade is left on until stopped out by the trailing stop or exited at the close of the market. (See Exhibit 7 & 8.)

Humphrey suggested that the method can be made more reliable by trading only in the direction indicated by the half-hour stochastic with 14 periods. For example, if the half-hour %K is above the %D, you would use the one-minute stochastic for buy signals only.

EXHIBIT 7

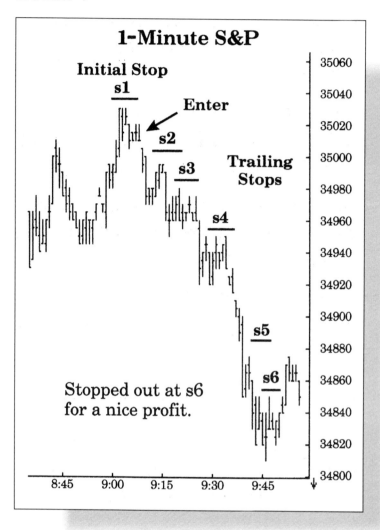

EXHIBIT 8

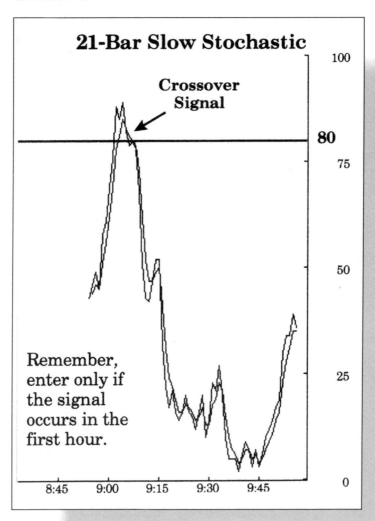

21-Bar Slow Stochastic

Crossover
Signal

Remember,
enter only if
the signal
occurs in the
first hour.

PIVOT POINTS

7

s we have explained in our previous chapters, we don't believe in the general practice of forecasting specific prices. However, if enough people use exactly the same method and wind up looking at the same forecasted prices, perhaps they do start to have some predictable impact on trading.

We suspect that the popularity of these pivot points is causing them to act as self-fulfilling prophecies. The formula for figuring pivot points (or support and resistance levels) was explained to us by one of our newsletter subscribers, Neal Weintraub, author of *The Weintraub Daytrader* and a floor trader in Chicago, who conducts some unique training seminars for traders, which he calls "Commodity Boot Camp." Neal explained to us that the formula is very widely followed, particularly by many floor traders who make a note of the pivot points before entering the pit each day. Neal suggested that knowledge of the calculations might be especially useful for S&P traders.

We start the pivot point calculations by adding together the previous day's high, low, and close. Then we divide by three to get an average price. Example:

Yesterday's high = 365.30

Yesterday's low = 361.30

Yesterday's close = 364.40

Total = 1091.00 divided by 3 = 363.66 avg. price)

Now to find today's pivot point high (or resistance level) we simply take the previous day's average price, multiply it by two, and then subtract the previous day's low. Example:

363.66 (yesterday's average price) x 2 = 727.32

727.32 - 361.30 (yesterday's low)= 366.02 (expected pivot point high)

Next, to find today's pivot point low (or support level) we simply take the previous day's average price, multiply it by two and then subtract the previous day's high. Example:

363.66 (yesterday's average price) x 2 = 727.32

727.32 - 365.30 (yesterday's high)= 362.02 (expected pivot point low)

These numbers represent the nearby support and resistance levels that for many years have been very widely circulated among day traders and floor traders. Since they are not chart points but are calculated numbers, the chartists will probably see them only after the fact, while the floor traders have the numbers noted on their trading cards.

Neal goes on to explain that we can carry the calculations another step further if we want and calculate a "highest high" (or extreme resistance point) as well as a "lowest low" (or extreme support level).

To calculate the highest high, we take yesterday's average price of 363.66, subtract the expected pivot point low of 362.02, and add the expected pivot point high of 366.02.

Our answer, 367.66, might be a good target on the upside if the resistance at 366.02 is broken. It would also indicate the next possible resistance level as the market advances.

To calculate the lowest low, we take yesterday's average price of 363.66, then we subtract the difference between the expected pivot point low of 362.02 and the pivot point high of 366.02 (a difference of 4.00).

Our answer of 359.66 represents a possible target or low point on the way down if our first support level of 362.02 doesn't hold.

We used real numbers for our examples, so we couldn't resist checking the S&P after the close to see how we did. The low of the day was 362.10 versus our projected pivot point low of 362.02. Not bad. (Sep S&P 6-21-90)

Again we caution that we think these points only work because they are popular and that popularity may be short-lived. If they should stop working for a while, because of some more important factors, they may never work again and you can throw this method away forever. On the other hand, if more people follow them, as time goes on they will work better than ever. In the meantime, we thought they were an interesting phenomenon worth passing along. We would be inclined to give more weight to the nearby numbers than to the "highest high" or "lowest low" calculations.

PRICE GAPS ON

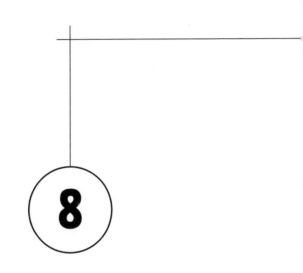

OPENINGS

A t a meeting of the Technical Analysts of Southern California in 1989, Bruce Babcock, Jr., was the guest speaker and described a day-trading strategy that he was developing. Bruce is the publisher of *Commodity Traders Consumer Report* and author of several commodity trading books. His book, *The Dow Jones-Irwin Guide to Trading Systems*, which has been referenced here many times, contains a great deal of useful information, and we recommend both his book and his CTCR newsletter to our readers.

Here are the highlights of the day-trading strategy that Bruce described to us:

1. Trading nearest month S&P futures, wait for an opening price that gaps noticeably from the previous day's close. You will then be looking for a trade in the

direction of the gap. If the opening price gaps up, look for an entry on the buy-side. If the opening gaps down, look for an entry on the sell-side.

2. Tack on a few points above or below the opening price range and enter the market on a buy stop or sell stop as the market begins to trend in the direction of the gap.

3. Use a stop loss of about $500 and exit the trade on the close. (See Exhibit 9.)

Bruce was probably intentionally vague about defining some of the instructions in specific terms. His gap strategy can be tailored to suit your individual trading style. Bruce indicated that he had done a considerable amount of testing with various gap and follow-through parameters. Generally, the bigger the gap and the more points you tack on to the opening range, the more likely you will be to have a winning trade. However, waiting for bigger gaps and more follow through means fewer trades.

Remember, profitable day trading requires high volatility, so we advise keeping the parameters toward the higher side, rather than the low side. That way you will be trading only after the market has demonstrated some volatility. As a starting place, try waiting for gaps of 75 points and tack on 25 points for follow through, if you want more trades make the numbers smaller; if you want fewer trades, make the numbers bigger.

EXHIBIT 9

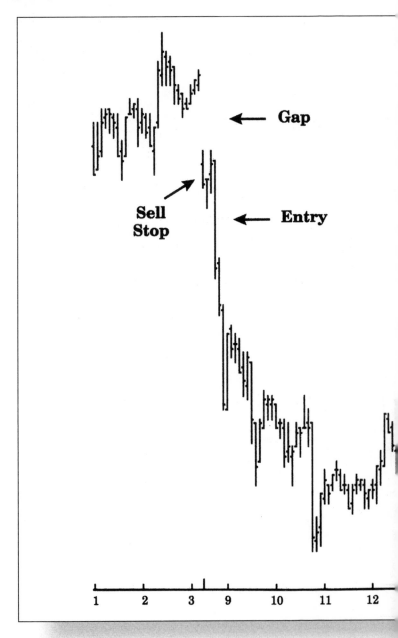

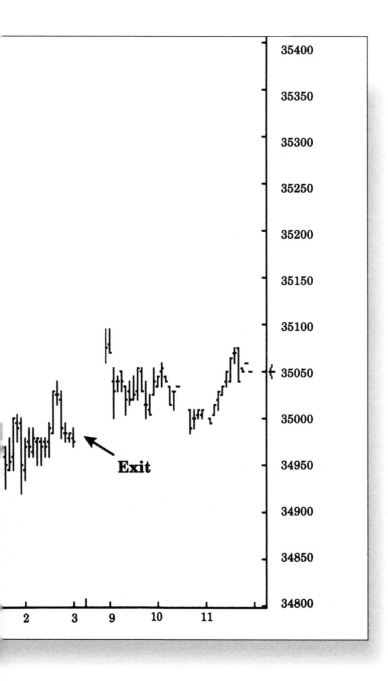

RSI DIVERGEN

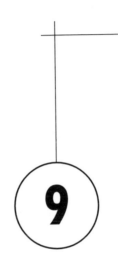

9

H ere is a simple day-trading method that uses a short-term RSI to find potential tops and bottoms in the S&P market. It is a logical approach that should work in any market and could be modified to use in longer-term trading as well. It is one of our favorite day-trading strategies for someone who does not need a trade every day. This method may go several days between trading signals, but, when the signals occur, it has a better winning percentage than some of the more active strategies. Since it doesn't trade every day, it could be a supplemental method to be followed in addition to a more active system. This method works best when trades are signaled in the direction of a longer-term trend. When there is no prevailing trend, the signals can be taken in either direction. You might want to review the use of ADX as a trend-measuring tool. When the daily ADX is rising, the day trades should be done only in the direction of the trend. When the ADX is declining, the trades can be in either direction. Be patient and don't anticipate the divergences.

Here are the specific rules:

1. Use a 30-minute bar chart on the S&P with a six-period RSI based on closes.

2. Look for divergence patterns in which the first RSI spike has penetrated the 80 or 20 levels on your screen. The second RSI spike doesn't need to reach these levels. Buy or sell immediately after the divergence is confirmed by a 30-minute close in the direction of the signal .

3. Use an entry stop of 100 S&P points or two ticks above or below a recent high or low, whichever is closer.

4. Exit at the stop or at the close of the day.

5. Don't enter any new trades in the last 45 minutes of the market. (See Exhibit 10.)

In markets other than the S&P, this day-trading method could be modified by changing the 30-minute bars to a shorter time period. If that were done, the 80/20 levels of the RSI might have to be adjusted to a higher or lower level.

It is worth noting that, in periods when the market is less volatile, 70/30 works better than 80/20, because the RSI doesn't get as overbought or oversold. However, one of the important virtues of this system is that it takes a fairly volatile market to make the RSI reach the 80/20 level, and trades don't get signaled unless there is enough volatility to make trading worthwhile. Don't be tempted to defeat that valuable feature of the system by adjusting the levels downward beyond 70/30 just to get more frequent trades.

EXHIBIT 10

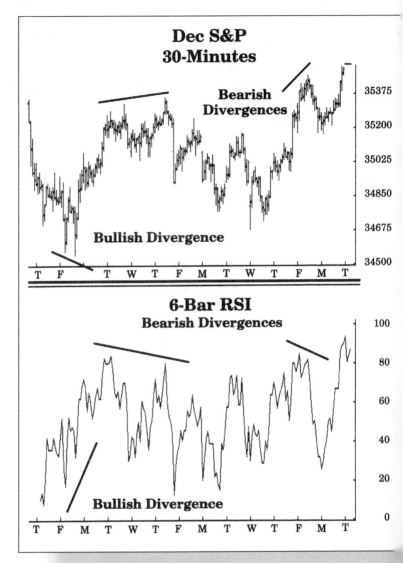

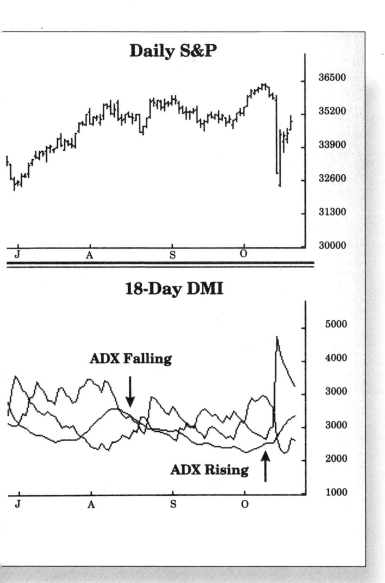

SIBBETS "KNI

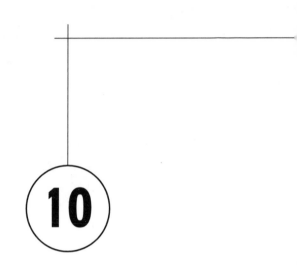

10

" SYSTEM

The following is a system for day trading the NYSE Composite Index (commonly referred to by traders as the "Knife," because it trades on the New York Futures Exchange). It is brought to us by our old friend and mentor of 25 years ago, Jim Sibbet, who is probably best known for his "Demand Index" and his newsletters on silver and gold. Jim says he prefers to trade the NYFE, instead of the S&P, because on a per dollar of margin basis he can make more money using the NYFE. He also believes it is a more orderly market with less risk. Here is his explanation of the strategy:

1. Use 5-, 10-, or 15-minute charts on the nearest NYFE contract. You just need price data, not patterns of any kind–so the time intervals don't matter.

2. Identify a fairly recent significant high or low point on the chart. (Just eyeball it for now.) If the point was a high, we will be looking to go short as soon as the market has declined by 0.70 from the high. If the significant point was a low, we will be looking to buy as soon as the market goes up by 0.70 from the low. Once the market has moved 0.70 from a high or low, we want to follow the current direction under the assumption that it's going farther. You should use a buy stop or sell stop at the 0.70 change in direction to automatically put you into the trade.

3. Once you have started a trade, protect yourself with a very close stop loss order at 0.30 from your entry point.

4. If the trade goes in your favor, as soon as you are ahead by 0.30 move your stop up to your entry point. As soon as you get ahead by 0.70 move your stop again to 0.50 points away, so you lock in a 0.20 profit. When you are ahead by 0.90, use a 0.70 trailing stop and be prepared to not only exit but to reverse the trade. (You may not want to reverse late in the day, unless you are prepared to carry the trade overnight. Jim will carry the trade overnight only if he is on the right side of his other indicators.)

5. If you are unlucky and get stopped out before you reach the point where your stops are 0.70 away, you

should try and re-enter the market in the same direction. On the re-entry, you will put the trade back on as soon as the market moves 0.20 in the direction of your first trade. (The fact that the market has not reversed by 0.70 since the previous signal indicates there is still a trend in the same direction you attempted to trade before.) Jim says he often is able to re-enter the market at a better price than his exit and make money on the second try. (See Exhibit 11.)

We were more than a little worried about the potential activity and market watching that is required by Jim's methods. If we go out for coffee we might miss two or three stop changes and a couple of reversals.

We would also need a very patient and understanding broker, one who would put up with the frequent stop changes. However, there is some basic merit to the system, and we thought it was worth passing along as food for thought. It might be the basis for a more practical system with wider parameters.

EXHIBIT 11

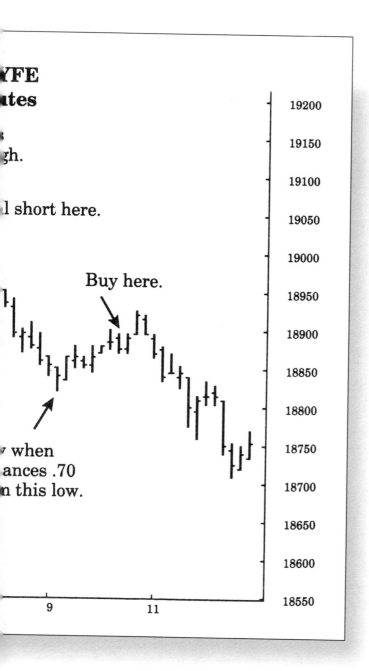

YFE
ites

gh.

l short here.

Buy here.

when
ances .70
n this low.

9   11

19200
19150
19100
19050
19000
18950
18900
18850
18800
18750
18700
18650
18600
18550

STOCHASTIC D

11

VERGENCES

This day-trading method combines the ADX, half-hour stochastics, and three-minute stochastics. This system works best in S&P futures and currencies.

1.   Use the 18-day ADX/DMI to measure the strength of the daily trend. If the ADX is rising, trades should be done only in the direction of the trend. If the ADX is declining, trades can be done in either direction.

2.   Check the direction of the short-term trend using half-hour bars on the slow stochastics as an indicator of the direction of the trend. It is O.K. to trade either with or against the stochastics trend as long as the 18-day ADX/DMI is declining.

3. Use three-minute bars on the futures contract. Set up another chart using three-minute bars with a 21-period slow stochastic.

4. Trades are entered after a divergence between the three-minute futures chart and the three-minute stochastic chart. The first point of the divergence must occur with the stochastic either above 80 or below 20. Look for occasional three-point divergences. These are less frequent than the two-point divergences, but they are particularly good signals. In fact, you can take the three-point divergence trades regardless of the daily ADX or stochastics trend. (See Exhibit 12.)

5. Set your stop loss. The initial stop loss point for S&Ps should be 20 points above the most recent high for short positions or 20 points under the recent low for long positions. The stop can be changed after each new peak or valley in the stochastics, with the stop 20 points from the new peak or valley on the S&P chart.

6. Take profits or exit on the close. If the three-minute stochastic gives a signal contrary to your position from a point below 20 or above 80, this is where you should take your profit. Make sure you are out by the close, if not stopped out.

EXHIBIT 12

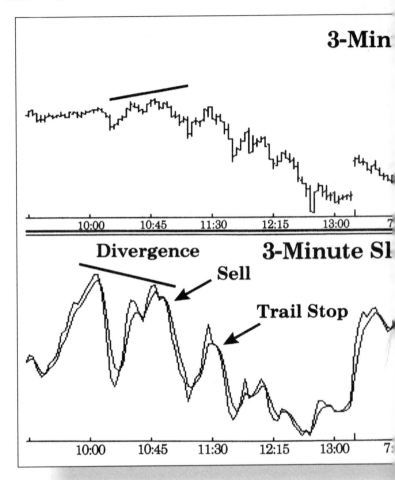

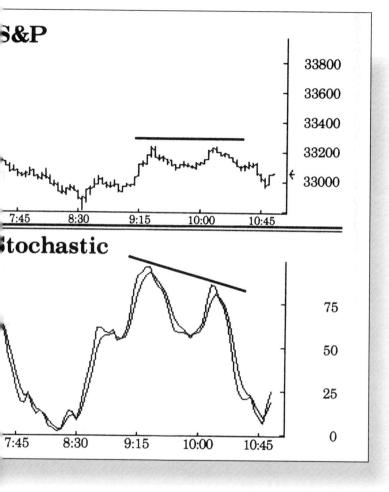

SWING REVER
PLUS STOCHASTICS

T his day-trading idea combines several technical elements: pattern recognition (something we haven't talked much about), stochastics, and divergence. We assume that most of our readers have some understanding of stochastics and stochastic divergence, since we've described them in detail in the previous chapter. However, the pattern recognition portion is a new element and requires a brief explanation.

The goal of pattern recognition is to try to predict market turning points by observing a sequence of price movements that occur regularly and that have some predictive value. The one described here is called a "key reversal" or "swing reversal" (see Exhibit 13.) This is a three-bar pattern with a swing low that makes a new short-term low followed by a third bar, which does not make a low and whose close is above the swing close. The reverse of this pattern would be used for identifying market tops.

With this pattern in mind, the trading system is as follows:

1. Use 30-minute bars on the S&P futures and a nine-period slow stochastic.

2. Watch for the short-term key reversal or swing reversal patterns we described above.

3. Enter the trade when you've observed a key reversal pattern that is accompanied by a stochastic reading (%D) below 30 for a buy pattern, or above 70 if it's a sell pattern.

4. Set a protective stop a tick or two outside the swing high or low. If this stop is too far away to be comfortable, use a tighter dollar stop.

5. Exit on any key reversal patterns in the opposite direction, or at the close. (Again, See Exhibit 13.)

Your chances for success will be greater if you wait for a divergence between the stochastic and the underlying futures prices. However, the divergence is not strictly necessary.

EXHIBIT 13

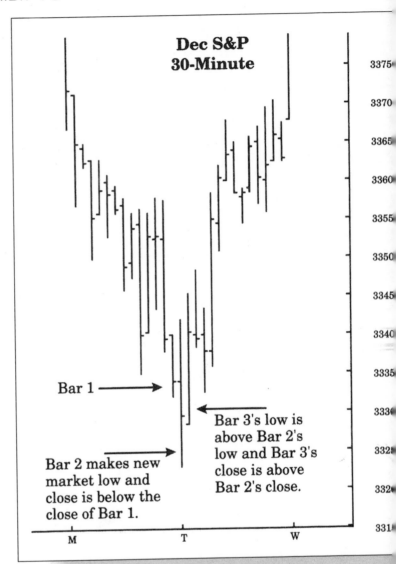

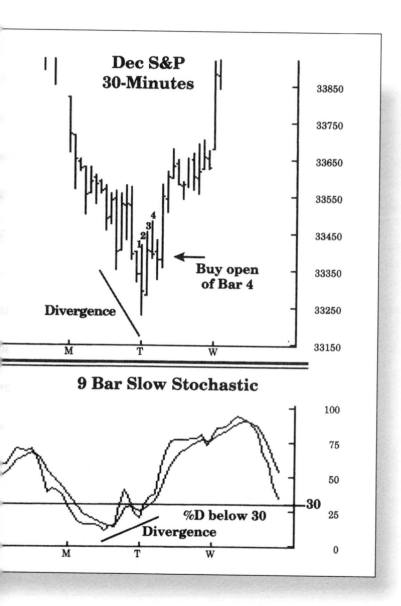

Dec S&P 30-Minutes

33850
33750
33650
33550
33450
33350
33250
33150

Buy open of Bar 4

Divergence

M   T   W

9 Bar Slow Stochastic

100
75
50
30
25
0

%D below 30

Divergence

M   T   W

APPLYING WHAT YOU'VE LEARNED

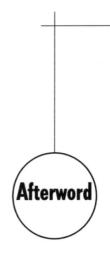

Afterword

by Jaye Lasine Abbate

USING ON-LINE AND SOFTWARE SYSTEMS TO ASSIST YOUR DAY TRADING

You have just been introduced to nearly a dozen different day trading systems and methods, and cautioned to use them with care. As emphasized at the outset, Day Trading can be a risky business. Because of the short term nature of the trading period, the tremendous volatility in the market recently, and the greater number of trades conducted which increases total transaction costs, Day Trading has often been a tough way to earn trading profits - though the potential for profits can be spectacular. A huge number of technological advances have occurred, though, that make it easier than ever to day trade. The critical information needed to do so is now completely accessible at an affordable price to anyone with a PC - rather than being available exclusively to the professionals.

With this in mind - the challenge becomes learning how to integrate these new online services and software systems with the methods and techniques discussed in previous chapters. A growing number of web-based and software products - including the CD included in the back of this book - offer a wide range of services. But which ones are critical to your success as a day trader? The definitive answer will become obvious only as you perfect your own unique style and method of day trading. However, the following criteria are essential tools for day trading success, and should be considered when evaluating any new system:

- **Quotes:** Good, quick and accurate quotes are fundamental to all short-term traders. Most day traders, though, require NASDAQ level 2 quotes because they show which market makers and ECN's (Electronic Communication Networks) are bidding and offering stock at what prices, which helps to indicate whether there is support for or resistance in a stock and what those support and resistance levels are. Additionally, through the use of level 2 quotes, traders may notice patterns in the market maker activity which, in turn, assists the trader in determining entry and exit points and strategy. One stock, for instance, may run up a half point every time the same three market makers are on the bid while a fourth market maker is not on the offer. So, choosing the right quote level to meet your needs is imperative.

- **News, Charts, technical analysis and market summaries:**
These are common elements of most systems nowadays -
and provide instant access to the ongoing research and
analysis tools you need to make quick decisions that capi-
talize on fast breaking market movements. Often, due to
a single news headline the day trader will be minutes
ahead of the general public - during which time the stock
may have gone up many points.

Likewise, charts and technical analysis tools can reveal
rapidly changing conditions the day trader can take
advantage of. For example, if Bollinger Bands are available on your system, they can be an extremely powerful
aid. Bollinger Bands vary depending on the volatility of a
security. As a security's volatility increases, the bands
will widen; as volatility decreases the bands narrow.
When the width between the upper band and the lower
band narrows, the odds of a tradable rally increases. The
direction of the resulting breakout is not known. You
can either use indicator readings to determine the direction of the move or simply wait until the move occurs by
placing the trade as soon as the security breaks above or
below a Bollinger Band. If the bands are close together
and the security breaks above the upper band, go long.
If the bands are narrow and the security breaks below
the lower band, go short. Either way they can help keep
trading losses to a minimum - as can other charts and
technical analysis tools.

Market summaries are also a useful tool for the day trader to have access to. Traders can monitor issues which have the highest percentage increase in price or volume on a particular exchange, and then research news or fundamental data that may be triggering these increases. The key is to sign up for a service that includes all these important features.

- **Portfolio Tracking:** The new technology is supposed to make your job easier. Therefore, any system you choose should track multiple portfolios - showing both your P&L and your positions, updating your account, keeping track of open orders and available buying power - and it should all be easily accessible to you.

- **Customer Service and Chat rooms:** Prompt customer service and the ability to talk to a real person when you need a quick answer regarding your account is a 'must'. "Chatting" with other traders to share experiences and information, and being able to participate in free seminars with industry pros, is extremely helpful and can lead to more effective trading techniques and decisions. Technology is allowing "professional" traders to come together in one location to share their ideas and "war" stories. The chat room, therefore, is now an equalizer - and geography no longer an inhibitor.

Plus, you should carefully consider:

- **Ease of use:** Dynamic screens, scrolling ticker, pop up screens, continual updating, and alerts simplify gathering info and are just a few of the elements that will make your trading easier and more efficient.

• **Customization capabilities:** Is the system set up so it's easy for you to obtain only the information you want, without having to sort through a lot of extraneous material? Does it monitor enough symbols? Does it cover all the charts you need?

Ask yourself these critical questions and others before choosing a system so you're not stuck with one that doesn't suit your trading style and needs. Remember: YOU must be comfortable with the system you choose, regardless of how many people may swear by one system or another.

Also try to determine:

• If the system is really safe and reliable, or prone to crashes and hackers cutting in.

• If it is compatible with any hardware or software, so you won't need to buy a lot of new products now, or down the road if you upgrade your PC.

• Can you run the system at home and at your office, on different computers, without having to reenter the securities you are following?

• If you need to leave the system running all the time to receive data on the computer, or if it is available on the quote providers end so you can access data anytime, anywhere, without worrying about missing a quote.

There are many similarities - and many differences - in the systems available today. But you should start with the basics noted here, as they will help you successfully implement the day trading systems and methods you choose to adopt from this book and other sources. For your convenience, a software CD is enclosed in the back of the book that will immediately allow you to get up and running, testing out any - or all -of the systems outlined.

We think this will be a tremendous asset to you as you improve your skills as a day trader. Take advantage of the free software that's provided, so you can learn to apply what you've just learned in the book with state-of- the-art research and charting applications. Once you've mastered the basics - you'll be ready to take your trading to the next level.

ABOUT THE AUTHORS

Charles Le Beau is one of the most respected names in the futures industry. As editor and publisher of Technical Traders Bulletin and founder of the System Traders Club, he is well known for his trading skills and specialized knowledge of technical analysis. He is a former regional futures director for E.F. Hutton and Co., and the founder and president of Island View Financial Group, Inc, which manages money in the futures markets.

Le Beau is a frequent contributor to all the major industry publications, and he has written numerous articles on technical analysis and methods for building profitable trading systems. He is also a popular speaker at trading seminars and conferences around the world, and has appeared in the United States, Hong Kong, Singapore, London, Zurich and other locations.

David W. Lucas is a recognized authority on computerized futures trading and the author of many articles on the design and testing of futures trading strategies. A computer expert, Lucas is the technical editor of the acclaimed Technical Traders Bulletin and was formerly a futures specialist with firms including E.F. Hutton, Shearson Lehman and Paine Webber. He is vice president of Island View Financial Group, Inc., where he is responsible for trading managed futures, and he provides consulting services to professional trading advisors, assisting them in developing, testing, and monitoring futures trading models.

Trading
Resource
Guide

❖

Tools for
Successful
Day Trading

SUGGESTED READING LIST

COMPUTER ANALYSIS OF THE FUTURES MARKET, Charles Le Beau & David W. Lucas, Comprehensive 'how-to' book for traders who rely on computers and the latest software packages to assist them in technical analysis. Learn to build and continually test a trading approach, hone it to near perfection and master 14 day trading methods to incorporate with your software.

312 PP $70.00 ITEM #2146

COMPLEAT DAY TRADER: TRADING SYSTEMS, STRATEGIES, TIMING INDICATORS & ANALYTICAL METHODS, Jake Bernstein, Everything needed to prosper in the volatile world of day trading. Sophisticated trading methods are combined with a program of disciplined risk management to make you a self-sufficient day trading pro in no time.

240 PP $39.95 ITEM #2284

COMPLEAT DAY TRADER II, Jake Bernstein, Picks up where Volume I left off - providing advanced trading strategies, indicator formulas and system codes, psychology of day trading plus powerful new insights for "intuitive" traders who create their own, customized systems. A great companion to volume 1.

232 PP $39.95 ITEM #8967

DAY TRADER'S ADVANTAGE: HOW TO MOVE FROM ONE WINNING POSITION TO THE NEXT, Howard Abell, Reveals methods for mastering the self-discipline needed to overcome routine obstacles like inconclusive/conflicting market data, debilitating emotions and ambiguous technical indicators and gain the self-control needed to make your systems work in this fast paced arena.

209 PP $39.95 ITEM #6142

DAY TRADERS MANUAL: THEORY, ART & SCIENCE OF PROFITABLE SHORT-TERM INVESTING, William Eng, Trying to adapt longer term analysis to short term markets can cause expensive mistakes. A top Day Trading expert now shows how to adapt your analysis to intra-day markets, listing 14 different day trading methods for equities, options and futures markets - all with easy to use tactics and 12 actual trading case studies.

352PP $79.95 ITEM #2281

How to Get Started in Electronic Day Trading, *David Nassar,*

Find everything you need to get started in this fast-paced new arena. It's all covered: A general introduction to electronic trading; differences among SOES, Island, Superdot and other electronic trading systems; Basic to complex trading strategies; Money management techniques for the electronic trader - and more.

233PP $24.95 ITEM#10262

Hit & Run Trading: The Short-Term Stock Traders' Bible, *Jeff Cooper,*

Delivers a day-by-day trading plan of attach for the rest of your life. It's easy to follow and you'll learn which stocks to focus on daily, where to place buy stops & sell short stops and the precise amount of risk you'll take. This hot-selling guide is your key to conquering the market on a daily basis.

165 PP $100 ITEM #5695

New Market Wizards, *Jack Schwager,*

Meet a new generation of market killers. These winning traders make millions - often in hours - and consistently outperform peers. Trading across a spectrum of financial markets, they use different methods but share remarkable successes. How do they do it? How can you do it? Schwager reveals their winning trading tactics.

493 PP $39.95 ITEM #2106

Market Wizards, *Jack Schwager,*

How do the world's top traders amass millions? This classic bestseller takes you into the minds of the greatest traders Wall St. has ever known. In depth interviews with key players expose every facet of their strategies, making this a classic investment "Bible."

458 PP $22.95 ITEM #2241
ALSO AVAILABLE IN SOFTCOVER $15 ITEM #2243

New Trading Dimensions: How to Profit from Chaos in Stocks, Bonds and Commodities, *Bill Williams,*

Introduces a new method of market forecasting that combines traditional technical charting methodology with chaos theory and psychology. Includes in-depth and understandable explanation, direction and analysis of oscillators, fractals, AC signals and more. Practice problems, case-studies and tips to get you started.

260 PP $59.95 ITEM #10105

SECRETS OF THE SOES BANDIT: HARVEY HOUTKIN REVEALS HIS BATTLE-TESTED ELECTRONIC TRADING TECHNIQUES, *Harvey Houtkin & David Waldman,*

Small order execution System trading (SOES) has revolutionized the financial markets - allowing any trader to bypass their broker and profit from intraday price movements on NASDAQ. Now, this unique new guide shows traders how to use - and profit from - direct access electronic trading, think like the most successful traders, and trade to maximum advantage every day.

256 PP $29.95 ITEM #10061

STOCK PATTERNS FOR DAY TRADERS, *Barry Rudd,*

Profit from short term and intraday price swings with the winning methods this professional stock trader reveals. Intraday trend trades, scalps, swing trades - it's all here. Great for novices and can help all traders improve their skills.

224 PP $95.00 ITEM #8855

TRADING BY THE MINUTE, *Joe Ross,*

It's the book that revolutionized day trading. Learn how a trading veteran trades intra-day charts. Chapters cover: Trade-Timeframe selection, major/minor entry signals, stops, contract sets, breakouts, continuation trading, congestion, 60 minute day trading and more -all targeted to squeezing profits from short term markets.

350PP $175 ITEM #2131 *60% REFUND ONLY ON ROSS BOOKS

TRADING SYSTEMS & METHODS, 3RD EDITION, *Perry Kaufman,*

It's the bestselling guide to trading systems - newly updated and revised with the current, cutting-edge material and a hands-on look at the good and bad features of most trading techniques and systems. Covers the latest indicators, programs, and algorithms plus an update on new equipment and methods for trading.

703 PP $79.95 ITEM #8791

IMPORTANT INTERNET SITES

TRADERS' LIBRARY BOOKSTORE - *www.traderslibrary.com,*
the #1 source for trading investment books, videos and related products.

CHUCK LE BEAU'S SYSTEM TRADERS CLUB - *www.traderclub.com,*
the premier site providing educational material and guidance on the design and testing of trading systems, a forum for members to exchnage information and ideas on systematic trading methods for futures and securities, and discounted prices on related products and services.

FUTURES MAGAZINE - *www.futuresmag.com,* filled with information
for futures and options traders, plus books, videos and dates of their popular trading conferences.

OMEGA RESEARCH - *www.omegresearch.com,* information on
Omega products, support and solution providers. Also listing of their free trading seminars.

WALL STREET DIRECTORY - *www.wsdinc.com,* the best director of
financial sites on the web. A comprehensive source that will help you find the answers to all your financial questions.

TRACK DATA - *www.tdc.com,* a supplier of electronically delivered finan-
cial data since 1981 - with several services specifically designed to assist day traders. Timely market data, financial data bases, historical information, data manipulation tools and analytical services are available.

BRIDGE FINANCIAL - *www.crbinex.com,* a comprehensive source of
products and services for futures and options traders. This "one-stop" site offers current quotes, on-line data, books, software products, news and information - from one of the world's leading financial information source.

OPTION VUE - *www.optionvue.com,* a great source for option trading
software. Visit the web site to view the on-line demo and tutorial.

CONFERENCES & SEMINARS

FUTURES WEST & SOUTH

Twice yearly, Futures Magazine Group presents 3-day conferences featuring in-depth presentations by trading experts, plus an exhibit hall showcasing the newest products and services for traders. You'll find everything related to trading in an intimate, hands-on setting that allows you to mingle with the experts. With tracks for beginning, intermediate and advanced trading - something is offered for every active trader.

For information contact: Russ Koehler, conference director
800-221-4352 OR 312/977-0999

OMEGA WORLD

The growing trend toward system trading is clear and OmegaWorld is the premier conference dedicated to system trading and development. Those willing to take more control of their investment program will find of wealth of information, along with workshops geared towards beginning and advanced attendees. Serious, in-depth sessions, exhibits of the industry's top products and latest software and lots of exciting events make this a stand-out event for all traders.

For information contact: 800-327-3794

TELERATE TAG CONFERENCE, FROM BRIDGE

For over 20 years, TAG (Technical Analysis Group) has presented annually 3-days of balanced workshops for new and experienced traders alike. Structured to give you a firm foundation and keep you abreast of the latest research and techniques, TAG helps you further your technical analysis education in a structured environment designed to teach. Learn to trade with confidence and get hands-on instruction from the industry's top traders.

For information contact: Tim Slater, 504-592-4550

NOTES

NOTES

This book, along with other books, are available at discounts that make it realistic to provide them as gifts to your customers, clients, and staff. For more information on these long lasting, cost effective premiums, please call John Boyer at 800-424-4550 or email him at john@traderslibrary.com.

.